C000081535

Car Boot Sales
A Sellers and Buyers Guide

Alan Coleman

Car Boot Sales

A Sellers and Buyers Guide

Alan Coleman

The **Hallamshire** Press
1998

Cartoons by Bill Kirby

© 1998 The Hallamshire Press

**Published by The Hallamshire Press
The Hallamshire Press is an imprint of
Interleaf Productions Limited
Broom Hall
Sheffield S10 2DR
England**

Typeset by Interleaf Productions Limited and printed by
The Cromwell Press, Trowbridge, Wiltshire.

British Library Cataloguing in Publication Data:
    A catalogue record for this book is available from the British Library

ISBN 1874718 57 1

Contents

Alan Coleman

Introduction

Alan Coleman is the operator of one of the biggest, and probably best run, car boot sales in this country.

Chosen by Carlton Television to represent the better aspects of car boot sales in a television documentary in 1997, he has been involved in the car boot trade right from the beginning and knows the business inside out.

Alan has written this guide to assist anyone wishing to make a success of selling, or buying, at car boot sales. Whether it be a one-off 'let's clear the attic' sale, or the beginnings of a way to earn a living, there are pointers here for novice and experienced alike and tips to point out many of the pitfalls that may be encountered.

Oldcotes car boot sale at Worksop

1. Who Can Sell

Almost anyone can sell at a car boot sale, there are no class distinctions and, from my experience, I can tell you that we have both sellers and buyers from all walks of life.

Car booting is good fun. You meet all sorts of people and a real atmosphere of friendliness prevails. You only have to see and listen to people, as they come in at the break of dawn, to know that they enjoy the experience, and for some it is now a way of life. The restrictions which apply to selling at car boot sales are not about *who* can sell but *what* you can sell.

We have strict regulations on our car boot as anyone who visits us will know, we try to run it in a fit and proper manner.

Items not allowed to be sold

No illegal goods of any description may be sold:

- No illegal goods such as firearms or dangerous weapons
- No illegal drugs
- No duty free goods, for example tobacco or perfume
- No alcohol
- No stolen goods
- No livestock
- No copy or fake goods of any description
- No fireworks or explosives

Some of these can get past the gate and onto the car boot sale, it is almost impossible to search every car on entry, so until the seller opens up and displays their wares you cannot be sure that they have been truthful after seeing the sign.

'Cheers Occifer'

Good and bad

Many of you will already have sold goods at car boot sales and some of you will never have been to one but may want to sell. To cater for both groups, I am going to explain all aspects of car booting, from tips for the novice right through to becoming a professional trader—many a car-booter has gone on to become a self-employed market trader. Also, for many who have suddenly found themselves unemployed, car booting has become a lifeline.

You are allowed to sell your own goods to make ends meet, however, if you are drawing benefits of any description, always make sure that you inform the appropriate authorities if you start buying goods from elsewhere to sell on, as this can be classed as being self-employed and you should, therefore, keep the necessary records as required. (I am sure that if you contact the relevant departments they will be only too willing to help.) You are allowed to sell your own goods without any complications but you may well find, after trying this, that you have found the income and enjoyment such that you wish to continue.

The tax thresholds are quite reasonable, so it would probably be some time before you exceed the lower limit, however, you must keep proper records to prove your income. I hope that by reading this book it will help a large number of you to earn more from selling at car boot sales, and, that many of you will go on to become regular, or even self-employed sellers. For those of you who are already selling I hope to show you ways of increasing the amount that you get for your goods. After all, the reason for selling is to obtain a reasonable amount of money in exchange for goods, and there is quite a difference between almost giving the goods away and getting a reasonable price for them.

Car boots have had a lot of criticism, most of it totally unfounded and much, indeed, coming from people who have never even been to one! Probably the main criticism is that it is an easy outlet for stolen goods but, in my opinion, anyone who attempts to sell stolen goods at a car boot sale must be mad. It is more than likely that at any reputable, well-organised car boot, there will also be undercover Police Officers and Trading Standards officers present, specifically on the lookout for anyone dealing in stolen or counterfeit goods. I have spoken with Police Officers on several occasions about stolen goods being offered for sale and they assure me that it is far easier to apprehend those attempting to sell stolen goods at a car boot than if, for example, they were to be offered for sale to the regulars in the local pub. Some criminals will use the excuse that they have bought stolen goods found in their possession from another car boot sale. The police are, of course, aware of this problem, though it can be very difficult for them to prove.

What is needed, is some legal form of proof of purchase from a car boot sale, but it must be easy to administer. My best suggestion in the meantime is that a purchaser should note the seller's vehicle registration number and/or name and address The police could then check the item back to the seller and, if all is well, the buyer would then not be charged with handling stolen goods.

'Will you take 50p for this mister?'

2. What to Sell

Everyone has something that is surplus to requirements. In the past, goods were probably advertised in the local newspaper or local shop window, but now, in car boot sales, we have an easy way of offering for sale as many items as we can carry in a vehicle, and all for a modest outlay. You also have the advantage of having potential buyers waiting for you to arrive.

'That's the heirloom sold, and the chair too!'

The reasons for selling items are many and varied:

- ▶ You may have simply grown tired of them.
- ▶ You need to realise some money and certain items are surplus to requirements.
- ▶ Someone in the family has died and there are some things that none of the family want. If the relative was elderly be careful that you are not giving away a family heirloom.
- ▶ You may be moving to a smaller house and have not got room for all the furniture in the new house.
- ▶ You want to become self-employed and make a profit on goods bought wholesale.

The list could go on and on, but what items are readily available to take to a car boot sale? Let's look at an average person's home and see what is available for a first trip to a car boot sale.

First, however, what vehicle is available to transport the goods? There is no point deciding on large items of furniture if there is only a small family car available. Obviously for such items we need access to a van or a trailer.

Most of us hoard various items of household goods on our way through life, thinking that there will come a time when we will need them again, but the truth is that we rarely ever do. Just go through your house, room by room, and you will probably be surprised at just how much choice you have. I will suggest for each room in question, possibilities that could be for sale, perhaps for some of the reasons I have mentioned.

Hallway

An area which can easily be overlooked:

- ▶ Walls: pictures, mirrors, clocks.
- ▶ Furniture: coat or hat stand, telephone table, chest of drawers.
- ▶ Ornaments: vases, plant pots, plants, dried flowers.
- ▶ Lighting: lamp bases, light-fittings, lamp shades.
- ▶ Floor covering: carpet, rugs, mats.

Already you can see, from just one small area, the potential of quite a few things to sell providing, of course, that you have good reason to sell them!

Living Room or Lounge

This is the room in which most people choose to relax, we can, therefore, expect to find items to help us to do just that:

- Reading material: books, magazines.
- Walls: pictures, mirrors, clocks.
- Ornaments: flower arrangements, pots and plants.
- Furniture: chairs, coffee tables, bookcases.
- Electrical: TV, video, music centre, radio, lamps and light-fittings
- Floor coverings.
- Soft furnishings: curtains, cushions.

Dining Room

Often many unused items are put away in a cupboard or sideboard in the dining room—it's worth a look:

- Furniture: dining table, chairs, sideboard.
- Ornaments: vases, china, decorative plates, candlesticks, picture frames.
- Tableware: cutlery, crockery, glasses, table mats, tablecloths.
- Floor coverings.
- Soft furnishings.

Kitchen

This is probably the best room in the house for items to sell on the car boot. It is an Aladdin's cave of saleable items:

- Electrical goods: cooker, kettle, coffee percolator, toaster, food mixer, toasted sandwich maker, extractor fan, refrigerator, washing machine, dishwasher, electric carving knife, slow cooker.
- Cook ware: pans, frying pans, wok, steamer.

You need to search every part of your property for goods to sell.

- Crockery: plates, cups and saucers, cereal bowls, egg cups.
- Cutlery: knives, forks, spoons, kitchen knives, ladles.
- Kitchen ware: baking trays, mixing bowls, rolling-pin, casserole dishes, kitchen scales, jugs.
- Stands & Containers: pan stands, spice racks, utensil racks, bread bin, spaghetti jar.
- Cookery books.
- Furniture: table, dresser, stools, chairs.

Bedroom

Again, a favourite place, particularly the spare bedroom, where unused goods lurk—under the bed, on top of, or hidden away in, the wardrobe:

- Bedding: blankets, quilts, pillowcases, sheets.
- Furniture: Bed, bed-head, dressing table, wardrobe, wardrobe, drawers, blanket chest, bookcase.
- Electrical: lamps, hair drier, radio alarm.
- Ornaments.
- Books.
- Clothing.
- Suitcases.

Garage

This area ranks alongside the kitchen for the number of saleable items it may contain:

- Hand tools: (for DIY and car) hammers, saws, planes, spanners, wrenches, clamps, screwdrivers, socket sets.
- Ladders: extending ladders, stepladders, ladder stays, trestles, planks.
- Power Tools: drills, sanders, planers, routers.
- Gardening equipment: lawnmower, strimmer, wheelbarrow, hosepipe, spade, fork, rake, hoe, trowels, shears, pruners
- Cleaning equipment: mops, buckets, brushes, power washer.
- Decorating materials: brushes, rollers, paint trays, paint, wallpaper.
- Fixings: screws, bolts, nails.

Some time ago, a neighbour of mine was moving from his house to a bungalow and came to me to ask if I would clear the remaining items from his garage, he said I could have them for the car boot. I went round to the garage to have a look. Amongst other things, there were about four tea chests full of old tools, most of them rusty but I took them to put on the stall.

Within minutes I had drawn a small crowd who were examining the tools and asking how much they were. Knowing they hadn't cost me anything I just guessed at a figure. The tea chests were empty after just two visits to the car boot and, for weeks afterwards, people were asking if I had any tools left. However, my neighbour had tinkered with cars all his life and some of these tools were hand-made for special jobs which would have cost a fortune to buy or to have made. The buyers, in fact, often told me what the items were for, so I at least became more knowledgeable.

I realised, after the event, that I could easily have doubled the amount of money I made. I hope that by reading this book you will not so easily make the same sort of mistake.

The Garden

This is an easily forgotten but useful source of items for a car boot:

- Garden furniture: table, chairs, relaxers, parasols.
- Pond accessories: fountain, pump, pond liner, water plants.
- Plants and shrubs.
- Children's Play: swing, slide, sand pit, paddling pool.
- Garden shed or greenhouse: (gardening equipment as listed under garage) plant pots, seed trays, cloches, canes, plant labels.

3. Preparing to Sell

Now you have an idea of the sort of items, readily available in an average household, which will sell on a car boot stall and you have already decided what to take along. You now want to make sure that the sale is a success, both in terms of enjoyment and by raising as much money for the goods as you can.

You can easily increase your asking price, and the speed at which you sell your goods, by making the items more attractive to the buyers. What I would like to show you in this chapter is how to do that, but first, I would like to point out one or two things that you should not do:

▶ Never sell electrical items that are faulty or dangerous. Apart from the risk of injury or even death for the unfortunate buyer, you could very well end up with a claim against you.
▶ Never sell items of food or perishable goods that are out of date and could therefore cause illness.
▶ Never attempt to sell any illegal goods (see page 9) the consequences would make it a very expensive day out!

Having collected your goods for sale from all over the house, I shall now group these items into categories and suggest ways of dealing with each to make your goods more saleable and, of course, get a better price.

Antique and Old furniture

Unless you are skilled in this field, you should never attempt to clean or restore old items yourself. If you have any items of furniture which you suspect may be of some value, then I suggest that you take them to a reputable auction house where you will be given a valuation and an idea of what the item could fetch at auction. This price, remember, will be a dealer's price, and car boots are now well attended by dealers looking for house clearances and items from old people's houses.

I had an old, studded leather rocking chair which I took to a local auction house, there they gave me a valuation which I said I would think about. I decided to take it to the car boot at the weekend where it immediately raised interest amongst three dealers. One asked me how much I wanted for the chair. Knowing that if he bought it at auction he would at least double the figure when he sold it on, I gave a price of one and a half times the valuation. He hummed and hawed about it, kept examining it, then put it down and made a bid below the asking price. I declined his offer, at which point, one of the other dealers said 'I'll have it' and thrust the asking price into my hand—much to the amazement of the first dealer.

I know now that I could have got double my asking price for the chair, but that is experience, and it is incidents like the one I have described which have encouraged me to write this book. I now have years of experience, not only in selling and buying at car boot sales, but also of organising them, and I would like to pass on some of what I have learned to others who are, perhaps, just starting off.

Electrical items

Remember, all electrical items must be safe. No frayed cords, faulty wiring or cracked casings:

▶ Clean: use a non-scratch cleaner for plastic casing. An iron will sell much better if the sole plate is clean and smooth. Make sure you clean out the dust bag on vacuum cleaners—there is nothing worse that a pile of dog hairs or household dust falling out as a prospective buyer is examining it. Make sure also that you clean the underside of any lawnmower, including the collection box, or strimmer that you have for sale. The time you spend cleaning up these items will be rewarded by a much better price.

and

▶ Tidy: coil flexes neatly and secure them with tape or string so that when you get to the sale everything is not tangled up and the goods look more presentable.

At most car boot sales there is someone with a generator who will let a prospective buyer try an electrical item out, perhaps charging a nominal fee for the service.

A good buy bye?

21

Well presented goods sell more easily.

Kitchen Goods

These should be scrupulously clean and some time should be spent washing *all* kitchen items including crockery and cutlery. No one likes to see dirty kitchenware and you are unlikely to sell any goods that are not clean.

If you follow these points it should help to increase the value of your goods:

- Wash all items that you can prior to setting off.
- Remove any stubborn stains.
- Descale kettles, coffee percolators, irons.
- Coil all flexes and tie neatly.
- If things are part of a set, if possible, make sure that the set is complete.
- Have the correct size batteries available so that any battery-operated goods can be shown working.
- Make sure that any perishables are in date and in good condition.

Clothing

In order to increase the value and interest in your items of clothing:

- Wash and iron all the clothes you can. (It is not worth the expense of dry cleaning, as it is unlikely that you will recoup the cost.)
- Label the size of the article. It is impractical in many instances to try on clothes at a car boot sale, but if people know the size they are more likely to take a chance on them fitting.
- Cover clothes in plastic bags, this will not only help to keep them clean but makes them look newer and more presentable.
- Try to remember the original price you paid for the item, it shows what a bargain the buyer is getting.
- Give clothes a fresh smell, either by including fabric conditioner in the final rinse, or lightly spray them with an air freshener.

Eau de Car Boot.

Curtains

▶ Measure the size of the curtains and the windows to which they relate and label them clearly. This gives the buyer more idea as to whether they will fit their window.

▶ Include curtain hooks as separate items in a bag. You can then make another few pence for them, or, close the sale of the curtains by offering to include the hooks in the price. If you have any tie backs or pull-cords these can be dealt with in a similar manner.

▶ Display your curtains in large, clear plastic bags, this will prevent them from being crumpled and creased. You can easily remove them from the bag to show any likely customer.

Carpets

- Make a note of the measurements of the carpet, or the room your carpet is from, and label it clearly.
- Make sure that the carpet is clean and vacuumed.
- Make a note of the type of carpet and the material: Axminster, Berber, twist, polypropylene, wool blend.
- It is a good idea to make a drawing of the room it fitted, include any cut-outs for fireplaces, alcoves and doorways. This saves you from having to keep unrolling it unnecessarily for everyone who shows an interest.
- Take along the underlay if you have it. It can be sold separately, or, used as a closing point for the sale of the carpet.

Car Parts

- Label all parts with the make, model and year of the vehicle that the parts are suitable for.
- Clean the items as well as you can. As with other goods, clean car parts and accessories will sell much more readily if they are not covered in grease and grime.

Garden items

- Deal with the electrical equipment as previously described on page 21.
- Label plants and shrubs with as much information as you can: name, variety, colour, height and spread, position.
- If your plants are not in flower, try to take along photographs or a book to show potential customers.
- Have plenty of carrier bags available for people to carry their purchases away.

By giving a bit of thought to the preparation of particular items, the price you obtain will be significantly more than if you had just put the goods in the car as they were and sold them for the first bid made.

Most importantly, you must form some opinion of the price that you expect to get for each item. You can make a stab at the price when you get to the sale but, as you will find out, everything happens so quickly that you may be hassled into a price that is too low. Every week I see this happen, inexperienced sellers come up against experienced buyers who will offer a very low price which the novice seller will accept rather than risk having the goods left at the end of the sale. Often the item sold will end up, just a few minutes later, on the buyer's stall at four or five times the price they paid.

I have found the easiest way to deal with this is to set the price at home before the sale and then label the article in some way. Probably the best method is to obtain a roll or sheet of the small sticky labels which are available from most stationers. They are quite inexpensive to buy and easy to use. Also, of course, if there are two or more of you at the sale, then you know the price without having to ask the others.

4. Packing and Preparation

The ideal vehicle for car boot sales is a van as it holds a lot more than a car and, if it is packed up the night before, it does not look as inviting stood on the drive overnight, particularly if the windows are blacked out in some way. I do not recommend leaving cars packed up overnight unless they are left locked up in a garage.

'Next time I'll get Pickfords.'

Loading up

Make sure, when you are loading the vehicle, that you pack it in such a way so as not to obstruct your view of the road when driving. If you have a roof rack use it, bulky items can be easily carried on it and, if it is a cupboard or something similar, other items can be stored inside, so giving you more room in the vehicle. Make sure your roof rack is covered to prevent goods getting wet and also to keep things secure on the way. If you have a trailer, use it to take extra items. You can organise your load better and, when you get there, you will have the extra room in which to sell (though some car boots may charge a higher fee because of the extra space the trailer takes up).

Last in, first out

Plan the way you want items to come out of the vehicle on arrival at the sale, and then pack them in reverse order. Try to pack the most valuable items in first so that they come out last, that way you can keep your eye on them when buyers are milling around your vehicle. If at all possible always have someone with you as you set out your goods, so one can keep an eye on things whilst the other gets them out. There are some dishonest people about wherever you are, and a car boot sale is no exception, in the confusion as you get your goods out there is a possibility that someone will seize the opportunity to steal something whilst your back is turned.

The first items to go in the vehicle are the largest ones. Then you can fit any smaller ones in and around the larger ones thereby maximising every bit of available space.

The very last item to pack into your vehicle is whatever you are going to display your goods on. The most common is a pasting-table, as it takes up very little room and raises items off the floor to an acceptable height for display. However, I personally prefer a large sheet of waterproof material such as a groundsheet, or tarpaulin, spread on the ground. It takes up a lot less room and goods will not be damaged or broken so easily if it is a windy day or if they get accidentally knocked. I also feel that it is easier to keep an eye on your goods—you notice people as they bend down to examine a particular item.

I thought you said 'we've loads of time' not 'they've forecast Force 9'.

Cover up

It is worthwhile taking along some clear plastic sheeting to cover the items in case of rain, you will keep your wares dry and the buyers can still see what is underneath, a cheap polythene decorator's dustsheet is ideal for this.

Wrap up

All breakable or fragile items should be wrapped in paper, or similar protective material, and then put into boxes to protect them from crushing and breaking. The value and selling potential is reduced to nil if they are broken or badly damaged.

Ideal transport for the car booter.

Money bags

Have something available to keep money in, either a cash-box or, probably the most secure, a money bag or bum-bag that fits around your waist. Make sure that you have a good float of small change and £1 coins. There is nothing worse than being offered a £20 note for your first transaction and leaving yourself struggling for change. Never leave your takings accessible in a box on your stall, or in your vehicle. People can see exactly where your money is every time you make a transaction and, when your back is turned, it could disappear. I am sorry if I paint too black a picture, but if I can make you aware of the pitfalls then I may prevent you from spoiling what should be a very enjoyable day.

Free gifts

If you put smaller items inside others to save valuable space in the vehicle, then, when you arrive, remember to remove them. I have often seen buyers ask the price of something, pay for it, then walk off and find other items inside which they took to be included in the price. What a bargain—but not for the seller!

Ticked off

It is a good idea to make a list of everything that you have for sale and the asking price. As you sell the items you can tick off what you have sold and enter the price received. This will help you to total and check your takings, and you can see if anything has been stolen from your pitch. You can also use your notes to help you price your goods for the next sale. Also, if someone mistakenly says that you have sold them something that does not work (people do get confused and forget from whom they bought an item) you can show them the list and say 'I didn't bring one of those. Sorry you have the wrong person'. Or, if you have sold an item to someone and they wish to return the goods, you will know from your list exactly how much they paid. You must be careful though not to be fleeced by dishonest characters.

Taken for a sucker

Through experience, I have learned a lot of the scams people try to pull off at car boots. I was on one car boot when a buyer bought a vacuum cleaner off a friend of mine. About half-an-hour later the buyer brought it back saying that it didn't work and he wanted his money back. My friend assured him that it did work when he brought it to the sale. Anyway, after some very aggressive behaviour and a stream of bad language from the buyer, my friend refunded the money and the buyer disappeared. My friend was upset about this and adamant that the cleaner worked perfectly well. It was only later, when he had time to examine the cleaner, that he discovered the motor had been exchanged for a burnt-out one. The buyer had seized his opportunity, on seeing the same model of vacuum cleaner for sale on the car boot sale as his own at home, to buy it, take it home, swap his own burnt-out motor for the good one, and bring it back. The 'repair' had cost him nothing.

My friend now insists that electrical goods are checked before they are sold and has access to a generator to test them. He also marks all his electrical items with a detector pen so that he can prove if they were from him or not, if any are returned.

Silver line in

Be wary of buyers trying to buy very low-priced items with a large note. Car boots and markets are favourite places for the unscrupulous to pass on forgeries and get as much 'good' money as possible in change. Many sellers are not used to handling money in a fast situation, so make sure that you know what to look for: the raised 'Bank of England' at the top of the note, the silver line threaded through the note, and the watermark being correct—check the note against the light. Some forgeries do have a watermark, but it is a very poor likeness.

5. Attending the Sale

If you are planning to attend an advertised sale but you are not sure of the exact location, make sure that you find out before the day. Tempers will be frayed if you get lost on the way and arrive late.

'...then turn left two miles past the pub, fork left at Coleman's Farm. At the T-junction...'

Early birds

The organisers of some car boot sales will allow people in well before the advertised start time. At the sale that I run, for example, both sellers and buyers start arriving before 5 a.m. though there is plenty of room for sellers right up to 9 a.m.

Make a date

With smaller boot sales there may be limited selling space available and you could be turned away if you arrive late. This would mean great disappointment or a frantic search for another car boot sale in the area. Always check the advert and, if there is a phone number, you may be able to book a place.

Dress up

Make sure that you are suitably dressed for the time of year. It can be very cold standing by your pitch in winter time but, in the middle of summer, you need lightweight clothes and possibly even sun lotion. One of my best sun tans was courtesy of the car boot sales—everyone kept asking which country I had been to for my holiday.

'I think we'll cancel that fortnight in Spain Fred'

Food for thought

Take some suitable refreshment along too, not everyone can face breakfast at the crack of dawn, but it is amazing how hungry you can get after an hour or so in the fresh air. Food will be available at many sales but not at them all, and it is not always convenient to leave your stall in search of a bacon sandwich.

A good sign

On your way to the sale, you will probably pass a few home-made car boot signs pointing you in the right direction. The amount of traffic should give you some indication of how popular the car boot is and, if there is a queue to get in, it is obviously going to be busy. Keep in the sellers queue until you reach the paying point and be prepared by having your money ready at the gate. The big car boots usually charge on the gate whereas many smaller sales tend to let you set up and then come around collecting afterwards.

Marshal arts

At the larger sales you will be directed from the gate to your selling pitch by marshals. They are usually quite experienced so follow their directions as you approach.

At most car boots, to maximise the number of cars, you will be parked side by side with other vehicles, as in a car park, and you will only have the space of the width of your car to sell from. This can be a blessing for one person selling on their own because, once the paste table is erected behind the vehicle, it stops the buyers from rummaging in the back of the vehicle. Some of the larger car boot sales, with plenty of land, will park you in lines, one behind the other. The main reason for this is because it is much easier to park the sellers, but it also it saves the land, which is often grass, from getting churned up by manoeuvring vehicles. This arrangement allows you, the seller, to have the full length of your vehicle in which to display all your items.

Sellers entering the car boot ground.

Vehicle checks

As you enter the ground you will see the line of sellers that you are going to join as you are directed by the marshal. You will also become aware of a group of buyers ready to pounce on your vehicle. They will quickly go around the vehicle in front of you and, after a quick check of what the seller in front of you has in their vehicle, they will swiftly move towards you.

These early buyers are the so-called professionals. They can quickly deduce whether your vehicle is likely to have any antiques or other items of value and, if they decide yours looks promising, they will set about the task of throwing you off your guard and trying to obtain whatever interests them at a bargain price. These people can tell within seconds if you are new to selling at car boot sales.

Avoid the rush

If this is your first time at selling at a car boot sale I would advise you to pull up into position as directed, and then sit in your car with the doors and windows shut until the next few vehicles have pulled in behind you and the buyers have moved on. You could even get out of the car, lock it up, and then watch what happens with the other sellers and buyers around you. This experience will give you some idea of what to expect next time you attend a sale and how the more experienced sellers cope with the situation. Either way, you are going to get a far better price by not being rushed into quick decisions. The buyers who come later are usually the general public, they are more willing to pay a much better price because they are buying for themselves and not for resale.

Show time

Once the initial surge of buyers has moved on, start to unload your vehicle. Place your pasting-table in a prominent position, or spread out your sheet on the ground. Begin to display your sale items, remembering to keep an eye on them as you do so. It is advisable not to take them all out at once but try to sell them as you take them out, a box at a time. If there are two of you it is much better, as one can keep an eye on things whilst the other unloads. Remember to watch carefully anything of value and don't be rushed into any hasty decisions.

Stick to your guns

When you start to sell, state your price and stick to it. If, after quite a few enquiries about a certain item but still no sale, then you may have priced it a little too highly. You can consider dropping the price slightly if you are really desperate to get rid of it but, if you feel that the price is a fair one, try leaving it a little longer, or even wait until the next car boot sale.

Who goes there

The people who attend the sale throughout the day can generally be divided into two groups.

Before 8 a.m. Antique dealers, owners of shops selling second-hand goods, semi-professional car booters, or market traders. All of these want items for resale and will therefore offer you a fraction of the true value of your goods.

After 8 a.m. The general public who are shopping for themselves and their families. They are willing to pay a reasonable price for anything that they have a need for, or take a fancy to, providing they feel that they have got a bargain. Also, the general public are in a much better frame of mind for buying, they look on it as a nice day out in the fresh air and it is enjoyment for all the family. Some of the larger car boots cater for this with rides and bouncy castles for the children, and food and drinks stalls providing refreshments. Do not be too dismayed if you have not sold much in the first hour or so, the prices paid for goods are usually much better once the general public start to arrive.

Titivate your stall

What you need to do now is take a look at your selling pitch. If you are new to car boot sales, the first rush of setting up with buyers crowding around you can be overwhelming and you probably paid little attention to the setting up of your stall. Now that you have sold a few items and the atmosphere has calmed down somewhat, take stock of the situation and look at your pitch. Stand in the position of a buyer at the front. Does it look inviting? Can you see all the items on sale without any problem?

The proper way to display your goods is to put the large items at the back and then scale them down in order of size towards the front so that none of them are hidden from view. Aim for them all to be easily seen by the customers, it is no good having smaller items lost at the back, or left unseen in boxes. Once you have set your stall out well and displayed your goods to best advantage, you are more likely to attract potential buyers.

Lucky dip

I have always found that a good interest creator is a big box containing all the clearance items you want to get rid of. Put a sign on it 'Everything 25p' or whatever price you choose. All supermarkets have what is called a 'loss leader'—something which is sold either at cost or, as the name suggests, at a loss. This attracts attention—no one can resist a bargain. All the major supermarkets run special offers and the technique is used throughout the retail trade. Why not incorporate it into your selling at the car boot?

As with the supermarkets, once you have got people's attention with these bargains, then there is a good chance they will stay and look at the rest of the goods you have for sale.

Pass the time

Now that you have some potential customers, consider how to treat them. Talk to them, pass the time of day with them. Put yourself in their position, think how you feel when you walk into a shop and the sales assistant either just stares at you, making you feel uncomfortable, or behaves in a pressurising manner and puts you off looking around. Try to make people feel at ease and comfortable as they come over to look at an item, that way they are far more likely to have a look at other things on your stall too.

A short 'good morning' or a comment on the weather is sufficient, then allow them to browse. Only when they show some interest in an item, perhaps by picking it up for a closer look, should you then give them a bit of background information about it.

Closing the deal

History lesson

If the item is old, tell them its history as far as you can; where it originated—it was your Grandma's who'd had it since she was small and it was her mother's before that—or whatever the story happens to be. If it is something which belongs to you, then tell them why you are selling it, why you have no further use for it now, and how much you paid for it originally. The more background information you have, the more chance you have of selling the item.

Closing time

All of this will help the buyer to decide whether the item is a good buy or not. If they believe that you are telling them the truth, and not just making it up to sell the item, then you are halfway to making the sale. They will now be weighing it up, yes they are interested in purchasing the item, yes it is in good condition, yes the price is right compared to the original price paid or the price that they would have to pay if they bought new.

By now, if you are going to make any sort of salesperson that is, you will have been receiving buying signals from the potential buyer. You must not ignore these signs and you must act before the buyer has a change of mind. Any salesman will tell you that you can either close the sale there and then, or lose it just by what you say at this point.

I had a few years in sales, selling power tools and fixings, I have closed some good sales by saying the right words at the right time and also lost sales by saying the wrong thing at the wrong time.

When I was selling, once I new the customer was interested, I would show them the tool, demonstrate what it could do, give it to them to hold, feel and try and then, whilst it was in their hands say 'If you were to order one what voltage would you require 240 or 110?' I would get a response either way, of 240v or 110v then, straight away, I would ask 'Do you want me to send you one of that voltage then?' and more often than not that would result in a sale.

So, with that in mind, look at your customer who is examining the item you have for sale. You can use any closure that comes to mind:

- Do you want me to wrap it up for you?
- Do you want me to show it working before you take it?
- If you take it I will include something else with it for the price. (Remember on page 24 the curtain hooks kept separate either to sell as an extra or to close the sale for the curtains.)
- I will give you my telephone number so that you can contact me if there is any problem when you get home. (Give a 24-hour guarantee if you are sure of the article. This makes the buyer feel much more certain of the item and therefore more likely to buy it.)
- The last resort is to offer a discount. This, though, reduces your takings and profit margin for the day. I would only recommend this as a last resort, possibly as the customer is about to walk away or is putting the article back down.

'Can you wrap it for me?'

Question time

There are a few things to consider when you are actually selling. Are you going to sell again? If you are, then it is not so drastic if you do not sell an item straight away. You can hold on to it until you get the price that you really want. However, if you are only going to sell on that one occasion then, as the end of the car boot sale draws nearer, you are likely to become more desperate to sell and more inclined to part with the item for a lot less than you originally intended.

Proficiency in selling at car boot sales comes with time and experience, just like any other activity. Probably, at your first sale, you will allow people to buy many of your items at a fraction of their true value. In fact, if you sell your items early and then go for a walk around the car boot sale, I am sure you will see many of 'your' items on another car booter's pitch at a much-inflated price! However, you will soon learn, and if you go on to become a regular car booter your selling technique will improve.

If you are not intending to sell again, you just want to get rid of your goods and raise a sum of money in the process. As soon as you have sold your items, it is only a matter of adding up your cash and making your way home.

I do not know of anyone who has ever sold everything separately that they brought along to a car boot but, if you don't wish to attend another sale, then to get rid of the last few items, the best thing that you can do is to approach one of the regular, or semi-professional car booters. Ask them if they would like to buy the rest of your items for an agreed price. This gets rid of your remaining bits and pieces and lets you travel back home with an empty vehicle and nothing to unload on your return—exactly what you set out to achieve.

Most car boots allow you to leave when you wish, although I have heard of a few that don't allow anyone to leave the selling area before a certain time. I do not know the justification for this, but the theory is that it disrupts the selling area when it is in full swing and makes it awkward for other sellers who want to go about their business without being disturbed. I suppose there may also be a possible safety aspect to it, because cars leaving, and weaving in and out of people during a busy period, could possibly be a danger to the public.

Safety first

Whilst on the subject of safety, I feel it is worth mentioning that, just as at any other event involving crowds, there is always the possibility that at some time a situation will arise requiring the attendance of the emergency services. Any reputable car boot sale will be prepared for such an instance and will ensure that a wide enough aisle is left between sellers to allow for the passage of an emergency vehicle.

You may feel that this is an unnecessary word of caution and that it is an unlikely occurrence but, speaking as an organiser of a car boot sale, it has happened to me on a number of occasions. We have always been prepared, my staff have been trained in readiness and, on every occasion that the emergency services have been called out, the car boot staff have always been commended for their fast response and the expertise with which they have got the emergency vehicles to the required position.

We have had to call the services for various reasons and, like all big events, have our fair share of people fainting or collapsing. We always try to follow a procedure whereby, if necessary, the person is taken to hospital so that proper evaluation of the incident takes place and any proper medical treatment can be given. However, had we not been prepared, one incident I recall would have resulted in severe damage to vehicles and possible injury to members of the public. A young boy had set light to a haystack in an adjoining field which was being used as a car park. As the smoke spread and rose into the air there was quite a panic amongst the public when they saw what was happening, but the staff responded immediately. The emergency services were called and, before they arrived, the staff had supervised the removal of all the vehicles close to the incident and were in position ready to marshal the fire brigade straight to the blaze. Considering that there were about 400 booters plus several thousand people walking about that hot summer day, the incident was quickly resolved without any injuries and without any damage to the surrounding vehicles.

Bitten by the bug

Back to the car boot itself. You have got to the end of your first effort and if it is was to be your first and last attempt, you have sold everything, got some money and so have achieved your aim.

However, you may have enjoyed it so much that you want to do it again! If you have not sold everything, save what is left and don't sell it to the regular car booters. You can soon have another look around at home for some more things to make it worthwhile doing another sale. If you can't find enough at home then ask your relatives and friends, often they will be only too pleased to have someone take the things away that they have been meaning to deal with for ages.

You have tasted the art of selling and have the money in your pocket to prove it, you have converted goods you no longer required into cash. A successful day!

The makings of a good day out.

6. Becoming Self-Employed

Selling on car boot sales can be the first step to becoming self-employed. There are no interviews or tests to pass and there are some very good incentives to encourage you:

▶ You can choose which days you wish to work.
▶ You can choose how many hours you wish to work each day.
▶ You can earn reasonable returns on your outlay.

The first step is, of course, to try selling your own items. If you are successful and enjoy it, then you may choose to consider doing it for a living. When you do decide to try to make a living out of it, do it right.

Plan ahead

What you need is a business plan to show how you intend to go about it. If you are receiving any form of benefit then you will have to inform the relevant office that you are earning money in this way. They will tell you how much you can earn before it affects your benefits, if at all. It may be that you do it part-time and tell them on a week-to-week basis how much you have earned so they can adjust your benefits accordingly. It is possible that you may receive other benefits, such as family credit, to make your income up whilst you are setting yourself up as self-employed. The best advice I can give is for you to go and talk with the Benefits Officer who will be only too willing to help.

Record sales

Keep proper records of your transactions:

- Where you bought or acquired an item.
- How much you paid for it.
- How much you sold it for.

At the end of the week, the difference between how much you have paid out and how much you received is your profit, but against this you are allowed to put a proportion of your running costs, vehicle expenses for example: petrol, car tax, insurance; and other items such as accounts books and stationery.

The benefits office will obviously want to see this, as will the Inland Revenue at some time in the future, so you *must* keep proper books and all relevant receipts. Both authorities are interested in your actual profit, either at the end of the year, for the Inland Revenue, or week in the case of the benefits office.

It will probably be some time before you pay any tax, everyone has a personal allowance before the first tax threshold is reached. Any benefits you receive will be reduced accordingly, on a week-to-week basis at first, until you reach the amount at which you can be self-supporting. Do not be afraid of contacting either of these organisations, they are there to help. It is in their interest for you to do well.

Where to now?

Once you have your business plan, and you have organised the book-keeping side of things, you need to look at the practical aspects.

Now that you have sold all your own items, where do you look for further items to sell? You can ask friends and relatives on a regular basis if they have anything to get rid of, but that won't keep you well-stocked, you have to start looking at different ways of obtaining goods to sell.

The first option is staring you in the face! Visit car boot sales and buy as cheaply as you can from any of the less-professional car booters who are willing to sell at a good price for you. The art of buying at the right price is something I shall go into in more detail later, but in the meantime, I will deal with methods of buying items to sell at car boots and also provide the information you need to become a self-employed seller at car boots.

Buy and sell

You will be starting off with a certain amount of stock of your own to sell. Go along to a car boot sale and kill two birds with one stone, by going to sell and, before opening up, looking around the other stalls picking up whatever bargains you think you can sell for a profit on your own stall.

The best time to buy, for minimum outlay, is first thing in the morning. Many people are at their worst at this time of day, not quite organised and perhaps not thinking too straight in the first hour or so after waking up. It is in this period when you are most likely to get sellers to agree to a silly price for their goods.

The next best time is at the end of the car boot sale, as people are packing up having sold most of the things they brought. If they are new to car booting, or just doing it to get rid of surplus items, then make them a bid for everything they have left. Tell them that you will use the items to add to your own stock but that, obviously, you have to sell to make a profit, the price you can to pay must therefore reflect this and be a lot lower than the selling price they were originally asking. You could also point out that perhaps the reason the items did not sell earlier was because the price was too high. Most new, or one-off, sellers will accept a low price for their last few items—it saves them having to take them back home.

Car boot sales are marvellous places for bartering and this is what helps to create the special atmosphere that exists at these sales.

'Pity he didn't take the table as well, Sid.'

Under the hammer

Another place where you can obtain goods cheaply is at auctions, the smaller affairs usually held in village halls or local pubs—not the Sotheby's type!

Most auctions charge a sellers and a buyers premium. This is usually 10% buyers and 10% sellers which, in reality, means that the auctioneer earns a fifth of the total made at the sale. Many of those held in pubs, village halls and so forth, do not attract such large crowds, and only a few antique or professional dealers, they do not, therefore, generate such high prices for the lots.

Many of these auctions are used by local people for buying and selling, they may not want to go to the trouble of advertising goods or standing at a car boot sale. There is often no reserve put on these lots so you can sometimes pick items up for next to nothing.

The auctioneer usually puts a fee on items with a reserve, so most sellers will take the risk that the item will reach their desired price rather than risk losing his reserve fee. Often, however, some items will not appeal to the buyers present on that particular day, I have seen many lots go for a fraction of their worth—much to the annoyance of the vendor who thought that their lot would easily reach the price they wanted!

Smaller items, of little value individually, are not sold separately but are put together in a box with other items from the same vendor, they are then sold as one lot. The box and its contents may sell for only a few pounds.

Lots to see

Get together a list of auctions, from adverts in local newspapers or local knowledge, and make a regular point of visiting them.

There is usually a viewing time, either the same day or the day before, when you can look at the lots and go through any boxes to see what lies hidden underneath that may be of value to you. At this point you should make notes as to what you would be willing to pay for anything that has caught your eye. Once the auction starts and bidding is in progress, stick to your guidelines and, if the bidding starts to go above what you have decided is a fair price, do not be tempted to increase your bid. You may well be stuck with the goods or have to sell at cost.

Bits and pieces

I find these boxes of various items a very good buy for resale at car boots. For a small outlay of just a few pounds you can fill your stall, making it more interesting and therefore attracting more customers. Also, because you have not paid a lot for the goods, you can sell the items off at very low prices individually but still make a good profit.

Buried treasure

I have seen some buyers at auction using clever ploys to keep the price of these boxes down for their own benefit.

"Sorry, I didn't realise there was someone in the coat."

They pull out all the items from the box to examine them prior to the auction, and then replace them with the best items first and the worst things on top. This means that any other potential buyer looking quickly through the box may miss the good items at the bottom and think its value to be very poor. Even when the auction starts and the lot comes up, the auctioneer's helper, or porter, will only pull out one or two bits from the top of the box to show to everyone. The person who has re-ordered the contents can now purchase the box at an extremely low price.

So, it is important that you view the auction and spend some time examining all the items that you are interested in. By doing this you will not have the inevitable disappointment of buying unseen and finding, when you get home, damaged, cracked or chipped goods which you will find very difficult to sell.

Rain or shine

I remember one auction I attended some years ago. The weather was atrocious and hardly anyone turned up. The auctioneer went ahead anyway and, as the evening progressed, items were selling very cheaply due to the lack of attendance.

The time came for the 'boxes of various' to be sold and, bearing in mind that it was snowing outside, not many were thinking of doing car boot sales that week. I bought 12 boxes for £14. I knew that I could hold on to them until the weather improved.

However, I changed my mind and went to a hard-standing car boot that weekend and, although there was still snow on the ground, the sun came out—and the customers. The boxes earned me £92 less the £14 I paid for them—a nice mornings profit of £78 less the petrol.

All I did was to put the boxes on the floor and as people picked stuff out to ask the price, I just kept it low, knowing full well that every item sold after the first pound received for each box was a clear profit—it was good fun too!

Professional looking stalls

Expert eye

As you attend more auctions, and get more knowledgeable and more experienced at selling, you will be able to pick out some of the more valuable items that you know you can sell for a reasonable profit.

If you have an eye for older goods and antiques you can make a very quick and substantial profit. Once you are more experienced and know what you are looking for, you can start to take a few more risks.

Put it back

When you first begin buying and selling then it pays you to re-invest the proceeds back into the business, or a least a major part of them. This way your business will begin to grow and it can do this in two ways:

▶ You can buy more stock with your profits, keeping to goods of about the same value as before and thereby increasing your range and the volume of goods for sale.

▶ You can buy goods of a higher value this time, you will not extend your range or quantity of goods, but you will have better quality and goods of a higher value. This should bring in the same amount of profit for fewer sales.

Either way, you reach the same end if you work on the same percentage profit across your items. Sometimes though, if you are relying on higher priced items, trade can be slow but, when you do sell, the profit is more and in one lump sum.

Scout's honour

Another good source of items for your car boot stall is the local jumble sale. All local papers have a section in which they are advertised.

Obtain a selection of local newspapers covering a reasonable area, make a note of any jumble sales coming up and plan your time-table to attend. You usually pay a small entrance fee but, once inside, you can buy at very reasonable prices.

Most jumble sales are run for a charity, perhaps the Scouts, or a local animal rescue organisation. The goods for sale have all been donated to raise money for this charity and so they can be sold very cheaply as every penny made is profit. The organisers generally do not want to be stuck with items left over at the end of the day and it may pay you to have a word with them to ask if you can clear all the unsold items. You may be lucky and find that they will give them to you for nothing, especially if you offer to clean the room up after they have finished. Jumble sales are usually one-off events and therefore the organisers do not want, or have the room, to store left-over goods; they are usually discarded or passed on to other organisations. Even if they do ask for a donation, you can rest assured that it will not be very much.

It pays to advertise

Yet another source of goods for your stall is the Free Ads column in the local newspaper. There will be plenty of suitable goods for you and, once you have got to the address in question, you can practice your bartering skills.

These adverts are an excellent source of children's clothes and toys which the owners have grown out of. There is a good market for these goods so, if you are interested in this line, make sure you get an early edition of the paper so you can be the first to ring. Don't forget that these calls are classed as a business expense and can go against your income.

You could place a small advertisement in the local papers yourself, asking for car boot items or for household clearances. These adverts more than pay for themselves and you can get hold of some good items in this way, as many of the advertisers just want someone to collect the goods, pay for them and take them out of their way.

Some of the papers allow you to advertise free of charge, so it is worth looking around but, if you do pay to advertise, remember that they are classed as business expenses.

Commodious money

Most of the house clearances you will get will be run of the mill and have only general bric-a-brac and other bits and pieces that the family do not want. After all, most families pick out the good items for themselves, or sell them individually.

Occasionally you may come across items that are too old fashioned for the owners, or they may not realise their true potential or value and so let them be discarded or sold. Often, with younger people who have furnished their homes with modern furniture, any older furniture left by a relative will not fit in or look right in their home. This can be an excellent opportunity and you will probably be surprised at how little you can pay for a house clearance.

Old furniture, and indeed anything from older people's houses, needs close scrutiny. I have heard of commodes containing old five pound notes, drawers having money taped to their undersides, even old mattresses having notes pushed inside the cover!

Unfortunately, many old people have a fear of, or a reluctance to, putting their money in a bank or building society, and they insist on keeping it in the house, sometimes in considerable amounts. They leave themselves at the mercy of the doorstep callers, bogus officials and other unscrupulous people only too eager to take advantage of defenceless individuals.

When you are removing articles from houses where old people have lived always bear this in mind and check for any hidden places where they may have secreted money or valuables. They may have been of sound mind when they hid their treasure, but they may then have forgotten all about it and not even told relatives of its existence. There may well be a reward for you when the 'treasure' is returned to the relatives.

It is worth offering to remove all the rubbish at a house clearance, as if you leave the place empty and clean this could keep the price you pay down. Many will be to rented accommodation where the keys have to be handed in within a week or two, after that, rent becomes due. You clearing everything will speed the whole process up for the relatives who rarely wish to incur any extra expense.

Leaflets

You can leaflet areas asking for any unwanted items. You should indicate when you will call back to collect any goods that are available.

You can use this same idea for specific things that you are interested in, perhaps furniture or older items. People will, however, expect to get a good price from you so make sure that you know the value of any items you are offered. If you make a mistake and pay too much, it means you will make a loss on re-sale—and you do not go into business to make a loss!

Follow your leaflet drop, as you have indicated, by going around a few days later to pick up. If you make a request for your leaflet to be left on the doorstep if they have nothing for you, it saves you hours of knocking on doors for nothing, it also means you can collect your leaflets up to use again, thereby keeping your costs down.

Rags to riches

The old rag and bone man of the past was a typical door to door collector of unwanted items, and what did he part with? At the most a poor goldfish! He would then sort through his acquisitions and either sell them separately or, if they were of poor quality, he would sell them as rags for recycling. The charity shops do this now, all the clothes that are left go for recycling and are sold by weight. This leads us to our next source—charity shops.

As you probably know charity shops are now amongst the biggest new occupiers of shops in town centres. Since the growth of out-of-town shopping malls over the last few years, business in the town centres has decreased. Many have closed down and shops have stood empty, the only way of letting them has been to charitable organisations who get considerable assistance with rent and rates. Once again, like jumble sales, they have been given their stock and are, therefore, happy to sell the items for a low price.

Visit your local ones regularly, you can pick up some real bargains and then sell them on at a profit. The charity shops are happy, they have made what they wanted out of the donated goods, after all, any amount of money you get for items that you have been given is a healthy profit in anyone's books, and don't forget, charities enjoy tax concessions, as well as very favourable rent and rates.

Trading up

I think I have now covered most ways of obtaining second-hand goods for resale on your car boot stall. However, as you become more successful at selling, as I am sure you will, and you attend more and more sales, then it can be difficult to find a plentiful enough supply of second-hand goods. You need to keep your stall well stocked, enough to give you a decent return for your day's work, you need to supplement your usual stock with other goods. It is at this point that you could begin to make the transformation from being a car booter, to becoming a market trader.

Buying and selling new goods, as opposed to second-hand, is quite different and I have therefore devoted a separate section to this. Some of you may, after selling both second-hand and new goods at car boot sales a few times, want to make a full and certain step towards becoming a market trader dealing in new goods only. Over the last few years the differences between markets and car boot sales has become less distinct and you are able to sell at a car boot as a market trader if you so wish.

'I've shown the wife how to run the stall, now I can relax.'

7. Buying and Selling New Goods

You have got the car boot sale bug! You have progressed from selling your own unwanted goods, through the various stages including selling your friends donated items, buying on the car boot and reselling at a profit, visiting auctions and jumble sales for your goods and have even done some advertising for house clearances. You now have a developing business and, due to your own efforts, you are earning a reasonable and regular weekly income.

Sales pitch

You can continue doing all these things and do well. However, like in any other business, you probably strive to do that little bit better and try to put a little bit more icing on the cake. It is a natural aim to want to progress. This is why, if you work for a sales company, you are set sales targets. They are usually realistic but are slightly higher every time you achieve the one you were set. Sales targets that you cannot achieve are pointless and demoralising to the point when you would stop trying. With most companies you actually agree the level of your targets because there is then every likelihood that you will succeed—not many people want to admit that they were unable to reach a level that they themselves have set.

New for old

Most people, regardless of how much money they have, want to improve their standard of living. So with this in mind, you probably want to increase your sales but, in order to do this, you need more goods to sell. You are now considering buying new goods for resale.

'Henry! Don't take less than 75p for His Lordship's crown.'

The art of buying and selling new goods is somewhat different to buying second-hand goods and the pricing too will differ. With any new goods bought from normal sources, the prices are very similar throughout the range of wholesalers. This is because the various wholesalers have all bought from the same importer or manufacturer and so the price has been set to some degree by their supplier. This price will be dependent on how much they have purchased, the more goods they take from a supplier the better discount they get, which can mean more profit for them or lower prices for you. This is one of the criteria for you to consider when negotiating your own deals.

Where can I buy?

Wherever you live in the country there will be, in the surrounding area, wholesalers and manufacturers of goods which are ideal for selling on car boots and markets. I include markets because both go hand in hand.

Manufacturers may not want to deal with you direct because the volume of goods that you will be buying when you first start out will not be sufficient for them. They will probably, however, give you details of their nearest stockist so that you can buy from them.

'A bulk order, indeed!'

Looking good

Before you approach any supplier or manufacturer, you need to make your business look professional. Suppliers will be much more likely to take your enquiry seriously if you turn up with a business card and a letterhead. In fact a lot will not deal with you at all if you don't have the latter, so this is the first job for you to tackle.

Go to a stationers or a printers and they will give you advice and the options available to you. I remember when I first started in business I used a local printer who, for a small outlay, supplied me with what they called a 'special starter's business pack'. This included a few each of business cards, letterheads, envelopes and invoices. They asked what information I needed on the stationery and then went on to design it, even including a suitable logo—it looked very professional.

I would advise you to get a few quotes for this job as there is a lot of competition in this field and it is surprising how much difference there can be between different companies. If you don't want to go to this trouble there are even machines, at places like motorway services, where you can print your own business cards.

Wholesale rewards

Once you have your letterhead you need to find the wholesalers or manufacturers to visit in your area.

The main criteria is cost, which suppliers can provide the goods at the best price? This will give you the edge over your competitors. Unfortunately, this comes only with experience, and it can take months, even years, to root out the cheapest suppliers for your chosen goods. Don't be put off by this because as you become more experienced in the art of buying, and to some degree it is an art, so the selling will improve and be easier because you now have a slight edge over your competitors. by being able to sell identical goods to them at a cheaper price and without reducing your profits.

To begin your search for suppliers look through the Yellow Pages. Throughout the country there are concentrated pockets of wholesalers. The more wholesalers there are in an area, then the more the competition between them and, therefore, better prices for you.

The nearest area to me is Sheffield, in South Yorkshire, where there are a number of very good wholesalers. Then, just a hour or so away, is Manchester which to me is the main wholesale area in the north for the kind of goods that I used to sell. There, at certain wholesalers once I was known, I could barter the price down providing I took a reasonable quantity. The competition there is so stiff and they are well aware that you can go around the corner and buy exactly the same goods.

At one small wholesalers I could get exceptional prices at the end of the month when he had to pay his bills. He openly admitted to me on one occasion that he was selling to me at just above cost price so that he could realise enough money to pay a bill that was due. He did not have to pay for the goods he was selling to me until the end of the following month. In other words he was using the goods that he sold to me as an interest free loan for about 10 weeks in all. When that bill wanted paying he would probably do the same again if he was short of money.

Spoilt for choice

Now you need to decide what sort of things you wish to sell to supplement your second-hand car boot stock. If you put some thought into it your decision should be easier.

You may wish to choose items that you feel comfortable with. For instance you may be used to using tools, either by trade or leisure, and therefore know a lot about them. If you are confident with your choice you will make a better job of selling. This principle would relate to many other items that you have used in the past or have a particular interest in, the list is endless and personal to each and every one of you, so I will leave you to decide what would fit into this category. The main thing to consider is what items are good sellers.

Consumable items for the home such as toilet rolls, kitchen rolls and bin liners are good sellers. You also build up plenty of repeat sales providing, of course, that the quality is good and the price is competitive. These sort of items bring you a regular clientele once you have established a regular position and people get to know you. Also, there is every chance that your regular customers may buy something else from the second-hand or new items you have on display.

Address book

Once you have decided on the type of goods you wish to sell, you then need to find a wholesaler who can supply them. I have already mentioned Yellow Pages, but there are also magazines, one such is the *Market Trader*, this comes out weekly and carries advertisements for many different wholesalers and a large variety of goods. They also offer a service of giving you lists of suppliers, and their addresses, for certain goods.

I have made my own book of suppliers of all goods, so that if I, or any of my traders, wish to find a particular item, then I have the knowledge to hand. I made it from cuttings and details taken from various adverts over the years. If you do the same, and cross-reference by goods and area, then if you are in a particular region you can visit various wholesalers to see if there is anything that you may be interested in.

Once you have a list of the wholesalers that you wish to visit then either contact them by phone or simply call in. If you are going to an area where there are a number of wholesalers it will not be a wasted journey. In my opinion it is better to call personally, taking along your new letterhead and card of course, and explaining that you have just started up as a market trader and are looking for a supplier. Tell them that you would like to have a look at the products they deal in and ask them to give you any relevant information on their discount structures and so on.

Make sure, to begin with, that you have the cash to pay for the goods. They will expect this at most suppliers because they don't know you and will not accept cheques. Most suppliers will be only too pleased to sell to you on this basis, after all, this is what they are in business for and they will not turn a new customer away.

Trolley ride

The majority of wholesale stores are similar to a supermarket, in that their goods are stacked on shelves, you select what you want and take it to the cash desk. There are however, quite a few suppliers who work on a different system.

They have a showroom with all their lines displayed along with their codes and prices, and usually a minimum quantity to be ordered. You will either fill in an order form yourself, or an assistant at the counter will do this for you. This order then goes through to the warehouse and your selected goods will be got together for you. This may take some time and you could be given a collection time much later in the day. Plan your time and visit this type of supplier first in the day, and the other type whilst you order is being prepared.

You will get an invoice detailing the goods and prices, this *must* be filed away ready for when you do your book-keeping. Before you file it though, use your invoice to price up the goods ready for selling. There is no fixed profit margin on items for resale. It is up to you to get what price you can for them. You may find with some items that you can make 100% profit, then again you may have to accept a very small profit margin on other things. It all comes down to experience and you can only get that by trying.

The 'in' thing

There is always an 'in' product on the market at any given time, this can range from a new children's toy, to exercise gadgets or fashion accessories. If you are going to get involved in the latest craze you need to think about your timing.

You can get in at the very beginning, before the 'craze' starts, at this point you are unsure how the article is going to sell. The price is set high, but demand can also be high because the product is new and, as yet, there are not many available. You could go in centre-stream when sales have been seen to be good and continuing sales are progressing well. The prices will have dropped a little by this point. Your third option is to get in towards the end of the craze, the most precarious stage of all—the price starts tumbling very quickly as suppliers worry about being stuck with shelves full of unwanted goods. I have seen prices fall so fast in different warehouses in the same area on the same day, that some traders have paid more for these goods than others were able to sell them for! So be very careful.

Great expectations

This is all part of buying and selling new goods. Don't expect to have to be good at buying right from the start, you have to learn the art of buying and that takes time. There is also an element of luck in finding the right articles at the right time and at the right price, the whole process is ongoing and, as such, you never stop learning.

New goods professionally displayed

Target area

After your first buying spree at the wholesalers, you may come away thinking that you have done very well and found some very saleable items but, as you get used to the area and find your way about then you will discover other suppliers with similar, or same, items at even better prices. I think the best way of doing this is to set yourself a target and, when you visit an area, make a point of going to at least one new supplier each time. Check out new and existing lines for better prices, that way you will be upgrading your buying all the time and be in a better position to compete with everyone else.

Crime watch

A word of warning to you when you are doing the rounds of suppliers. One of my friends suffered a substantial loss when, having already been to two suppliers, he came out of the third and on returning to his van to load up, found the vehicle, and the goods, gone. The vehicle was found abandoned a few streets away, but of course, minus the goods. This is not uncommon, criminals follow vehicles from supplier to supplier and take their chance while you are in the store buying more goods.

Quite a few of the larger suppliers have either security or CCTV on their car parks, even so keep an eye on your goods and vehicle to prevent spoiling your day and losing your hard-earned money.

Consumer care

As I have already mentioned, you may choose to concentrate on selling a specialised range of items on your stall. Your other choice is to buy across the range including consumables that buyers come back for week after week. This gives you base average sales which should, hopefully, grow week by week because, once you have got regular customers buying your consumables, the sales are established and you can then build on them and increase your sales by selling extra goods as well as the consumables. You can also make it more interesting by having certain lines that change each week. This encourages your customers to look at what you have to offer that is new. When you deal in various lines like this and buy goods that are not of a specialised nature, but are really anything that has been bought at a good price, the market term that covers the goods is 'swag'

The only trouble with dealing in swag is that a lot of markets will only allow a limited number of traders selling the same type of goods. This is, I feel, a good thing because otherwise the market ends up sharing the proceeds out amongst too many traders on one type of product with none of them making a reasonable profit. They will move elsewhere and instead of having a regular trading base you end up with one that is ever-changing.

Check first before you go spending a lot of money on items that you may not be able to offer for sale. It may well be that if you work a number of markets throughout the week you may have to leave different lines off at some markets but, over the week, you can still sell the range of goods overall. Car boots are somewhat different, with not as many rules, except for the legal ones, and those of the individual operator.

Hopefully, you should now have some idea of what goods to sell on your stall. Whatever this happens to be I would advise you to buy only a few lines initially and build up gradually. In this way you can test the water, without too much outlay, and build your new business accordingly.

8. Buying from Car Boot Sales

There are many reasons for buying from car boot sales. There are many different types of people who buy from car boot sales.

▶ You are buying for your own personal use and want a bargain. You may be buying for your home or family
▶ You are buying to make a little extra money for yourself. You will sell the goods on again, perhaps at car boot sales.
▶ You are a dealer in antiques or second-hand goods. You are on the lookout for anything, in either category, that you can sell on at a profit.

If you are buying for your own personal use, then only you know what you are looking for. What will look right in your home, what suits your particular taste and what sort of price you are prepared to pay.

If you happen to be an antique dealer, or a dealer in other older goods or collectables, then obviously I am not going to attempt to tell you how to go about your job—you will be far more knowledgeable than I am. This book is aimed at helping people to get the best out of selling at car boot sales and also to assist those who wish to earn a living selling and buying at such events.

Down to basics

Whatever your reasons for buying from car boot sales, certain basic principles apply. Once you have found out where the car boot sale is, and how to get there, make sure you are there early so that you get a chance of the goods as the seller gets them out of the car. However, you will not be on your own, there will be other early birds competing with you. Keep your cool! I have seen some buyers become very irate when another gets a good item before they had the chance, even resorting to pushing and shoving when the seller first opens the boot up. It is totally unnecessary and can spoil what should be a pleasant day out for both sellers and buyers.

More for less

There is a skill in buying at the right price and quite a lot of people barter at car boot sales, just as you would find at flea markets whilst on holiday abroad. It is surprising how many sellers are prepared to come down in price, especially if they only intend to stand once.

If you are buying with the intention of selling on at a profit, then almost everything on offer is a potential buy for you. You need to be able to recognise a saleable item at the right price for you to make a profit on it. Try to get the item at the lowest price possible and, if there are a few items that you are interested in, make a combined offer for the lot. This will often work because the seller is happy to get rid of a few items all at once.

Make sure, before you buy in large quantities, that you have somewhere to store the goods, particularly if you are tempted to buy any larger items, until you are able to sell them at the price you want.

How much?

It is important to keep a record of the price you pay for each piece. Not only do you need the information for book-keeping purposes, but it will help you to price your goods for re-sale with a margin for profit. Also, as it could be some time before you do sell the item, you will not forget how much you paid for it and sell it at a loss!

A snag

When buying goods be very critical of their condition, examine them for chips, cracks, marks, wear, in fact any imperfections that would affect your re-sale price. This applies even if you are buying for yourself. On clothes look for any pulls, tears or snags and hold the garment up to see if it looks about the size it says on the label. There is nothing more disappointing than to get home and find your bargain does not fit or that it has a pull in the fabric.

After a while you will gain experience in buying at car boots. You have to be very quick when the sellers are arriving but, as the day goes on, you are buying with the general public and can therefore spend more time examining items carefully.

Honest and true?

Always avoid buying from anyone whom you suspect may not be the rightful owner of the goods offered for sale. To do so may land you in trouble with the law.

Most of the people that you will come across are honest and trustworthy, it is just a small minority that may have obtained goods from dubious sources. However, do as I advised earlier, note down the vehicle registration number of any stallholder you buy from, not forgetting to enter this in your book next to the item purchased. It could be vital information for you, or the authorities, if you are ever questioned about a particular item in your possession.

'It's a cancelled order from Rolex.'

Nice car

If you are buying first thing as the sellers arrive, there will be a few buyers milling around each car as it pulls up. If the cars are arriving quickly, a good tip is to let the other buyers all look at the first one and for you to move on to the car behind, or the one which looks most promising. You will soon learn to judge which cars are most likely to have the best items.

Look at the occupants of the vehicles as they pull up, you soon become experienced at working out which are regular sellers and which are new to car booting. Other tell-tale signs are the actual vehicles themselves and of course, with saloon cars and hatchbacks, you can see the goods before the car even stops. If you do see something you want then stick with that vehicle so that you are the first in line when it opens up, *but please be polite and respect the seller's property.*

'I didn't think our Enid's lamp would be so popular.'

Bagged up

A very useful accessory for you is a large sturdy bag or even a shopping trolley. It will save you numerous trips back to the car park, during which you would be missing out on things as other sellers arrive.

I spy

When you are looking at the items on offer, if you see anything that looks old but you are not sure exactly what it is, it could be worth the risk of buying if the seller does not want too much. Old items will often sell easily and sometimes for a lot more than you paid for them.

It is more than likely that there will be some antique dealers, or dealers in older second-hand goods at the car boot sale. Obviously they know what they are doing, it is their livelihood. If you can recognise who these dealers are, then you may learn from watching them. What sort of goods appeal to them, what they are prepared to pay. It will give you an idea of the type of goods you could look out for if you have an interest in this field.

If you are a novice at recognising antiques I would advise you to buy one or two books on the subject, there are several general antiques guides covering household items, including small items of furniture. Personally, I would not bother with larger items of furniture, they are impractical to transport to a car boot sale and are not the usual type of goods found there.

The guides will show you items that may be seen from time to time at car boot sales and will help you to recognise goods which can earn you good profits.

Great expectations

I would suggest that you go about your early car boot days by following the advice already given. This will give you a regular income and you will gradually improve your selling and buying techniques. All the time, of course, gaining knowledge from observation of other buyers and sellers around you. Don't expect to become an expert overnight, it will not happen!

Collectable items on display.

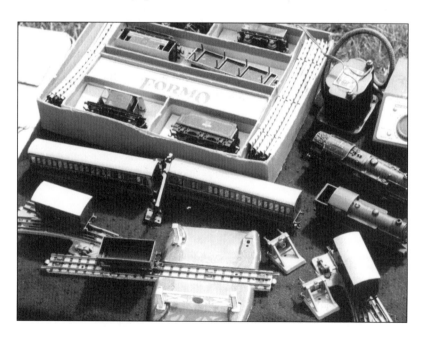

Premier league

As you begin to recognise antiques and collectables then you are entering a different league. Once you have goods that fit into this category you can start asking much better prices. You may well come across such items if you advertise for house clearances.

Always remember if you are unsure about the worth of something you have acquired, to get an independent valuation. This will give you a guideline as to its value before you attempt to sell. You may even approach the larger auction houses that specialise in the sale of antiques.

Up market

If you have a particular interest in this field, you can make the transition from selling the more normal type of car boot merchandise to selling old, collectable, and antique goods.

Both of these can run hand-in-hand to start with as, initially, you will have only one or two items in this category and it will take you some time to build up a stock of similar nature. Do not expect to do that well with them at first, as the odd antique on your stall will not fetch as good a price as on one that is specialised. Buyers will assume that you have it by chance and do not know its proper value and, if they think that you are a novice and not an antique dealer, they will try to knock the price right down.

The knowledge

Stalls that are full of collectables or antiques will help to ensure that prices are much higher—you will be taken to be an expert.

Therefore, when you talk to a customer you must know about the item that you are trying to sell, if you don't and the customer has some knowledge of the subject, then, not only will you will lose your credibility, but they will get your goods at a bargain price and you will lose your profit.

Never tell lies about your wares and do not deliberately mislead your customers. Until you gain experience and knowledge it may be better to keep quiet and say nothing rather than let an experienced buyer know that you are talking rubbish. In some instances it could pay you to admit that you are unsure of an item, you could learn from the buyer—*but be careful as you could easily be tricked into thinking the item is of little worth.*

'It's early Victorian with Queen Anne legs, madam.'

Index linked

There are numerous books on antiques and collectables, you need the most up to date ones available for current prices. If you cannot afford them, try the local library, you can then take them home and study them at leisure.

Using the books to help you, design and make your own reference guide. Use a loose-leaf folder, or an indexed book so that you can add to it when you want. I categorise mine under headings such as:

Books

Chairs

Coins

Dolls

Furniture

Jewellery

Pottery

Silverware

In each category I write down the names of the most notable manufacturers and producers of each type of product. This helps me to recognise good quality items and often whether the item is genuine or not.

You must sit down and read as many books on the subject as you possibly can if you are to become a successful dealer. It is also important that you see examples of these articles for yourself. Visit any antique shops and fairs that you come across on your travels.

All manner of valuable goods turn up from time to time at car boot sales. Perhaps a rare doll, a piece of collectable Art Deco, or a painting by a sought after artist, but you need some knowledge to help you to spot these articles when they do turn up.

Keep it brief

The more time that you spend reading books and getting to know the subject, the easier it will be for you to decide whether to buy or not and at what price. However, keep the notes in your personal guide concise, as in the bustle of the car boot sale, you do not have a lot of time to make up your mind.

Hold on

If you do see something of interest and there are other buyers around, do not let go of the item in question until you have made your decision whether to buy or not. If you put it down to think about it or to check in your guide you could miss out on a good buy.

One step at a time

Don't be put off by the plethora of information, it is a vast subject area but it can be broken down into categories and you do not have to learn it all in one go. Indeed you may choose to specialise in just one, or maybe two, areas. In any event, you will soon get to know many of the names and find that you spend less and less time consulting your notes. Remember, even the experts need to consult books, or other experts more knowledgeable than themselves on a particular subject.

Once you have looked through a few books you will start to recognise pieces from different periods, such as Edwardian, Jacobean or Victorian, each have their own characteristics which make them easily recognisable to the discerning eye. The more homework you do, whether this be reading, or watching the experts, the better you will become at spotting a good buy when you see it. This is true no matter what type of goods you are looking to buy and the better you are at buying the more profit you can make when it comes to selling.

I hope that this guide will have helped you to know what to expect when attending car boot sales, whether it be as a seller or as a buyer, and I would like to wish you every success in your ventures, at whatever level you choose to get involved. I hope you have many enjoyable times.